Pebble® Plus

Animal Groups

A Pack of Wolves

by Martha E. H. Rustad

PEBBLE
a capstone imprint

6/17/20
6.95

D1127039

Pebble Plus is published by Pebble, 1710 Roe Crest Drive, North Mankato, Minnesota 56003 www.mycapstone.com

Copyright © 2020 by Pebble, a Capstone imprint. All rights reserved. No part of this publication may be reproduced in whole or in part, or stored in a retrieval system, or transmitted in any form or by any means, electronic, mechanical, photocopying, recording, or otherwise, without written permission of the publisher.

Library of Congress Cataloging-in-Publication Data
Names: Rustad, Martha E. H. (Martha Elizabeth Hillman), 1975- author.
Title: A pack of wolves / by Martha E.H. Rustad.
Description: North Mankato, Minnesota : Pebble, [2020] | Series: Animal groups | Includes bibliographical references and index. | Audience: Age 5-7. | Audience: K to Grade 3.
Identifiers: LCCN 2019003025 | ISBN 9781977109507 (library binding) | ISBN 9781977110466 (paperback) | ISBN 9781977109569 (ebook pdf)
Subjects: LCSH: Wolves—Behavior—Juvenile literature. | Social behavior in animals—Juvenile literature.
Classification: LCC QL737.C22 R8694 2020 | DDC 599.77156—dc23
LC record available at https://lccn.loc.gov/2019003025

Editorial Credits
Abby Colich, editor; Tracy McCabe, designer; Eric Gohl, media researcher; Kathy McColley, production specialist

Photo Credits
Alamy: Design Pics Inc, 9, National Geographic Image Collection, 13; iStockphoto: Andyworks, back cover (bottom), 19, 21, Johny87, 7; Shutterstock: Bildagentur Zoonar GmbH, back cover (top), 17, Geoffrey Kuchera, 15, Igor Lushchay, background, Jim Cumming, cover, 1, Michael Roeder, 5, Ronald Wittek, 11

All internet sites appearing in back matter were available and accurate when this book was sent to press.

Note to Parents and Teachers

The Animal Groups set supports national science standards related to life science. This book describes and illustrates life in a pack of wolves. The images support early readers in understanding the text. The repetition of words and phrases helps early readers learn new words. This book also introduces early readers to subject-specific vocabulary words, which are defined in the Glossary section. Early readers may need assistance to read some words and to use the Table of Contents, Glossary, Read More, Internet Sites, Critical Thinking Questions, and Index sections of the book.

Printed and bound in China.
1654

Table of Contents

What Is a Pack?

Howl! Howl! What's that sound? It's a group of wolves! Wolves live in groups of about six to ten. A group of wolves is called a pack.

3 4873 00556 3077

5

A pack has one grown male and female. They are the leads. Their young live with them. The pack lives and hunts in the same area. This is its territory.

Wolf Pups Grow

Spring is here! A female moves
to a den. She has four to six pups.
They drink milk from her body.
After a few weeks, they leave
the den.

The whole pack cares
for the pups. Pups stay
with the pack for about two years.
Then they find a new territory.
They form a new pack.

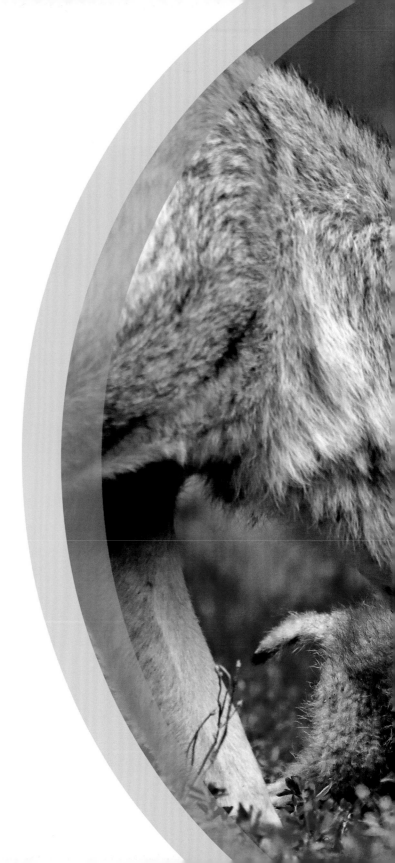

Time to Hunt

Wolves hunt deer, elk, and other animals. Each wolf has a job. Faster wolves chase prey. Stronger wolves kill prey. Younger wolves watch and learn.

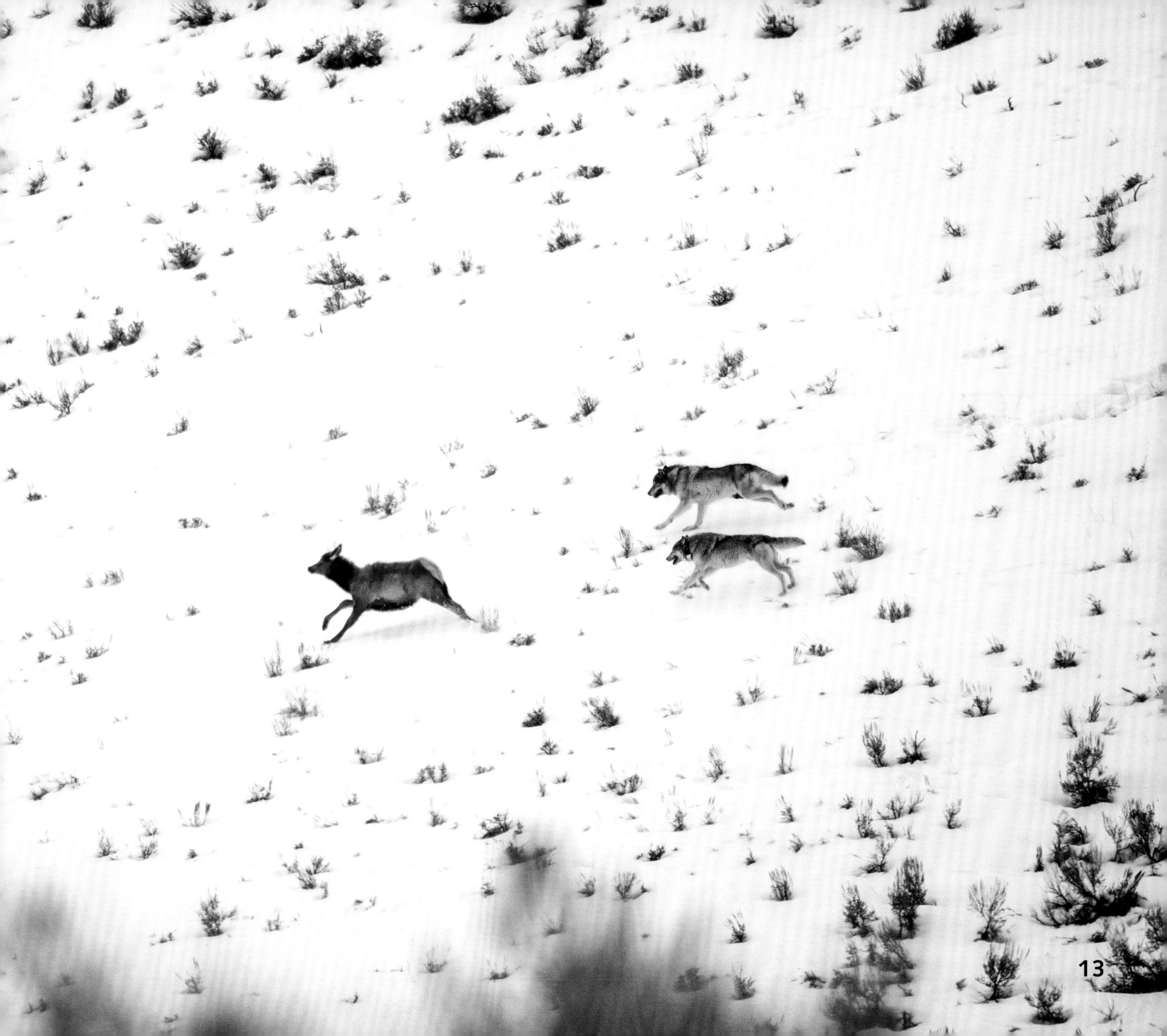

The pack takes down prey together. Sharp teeth grab the animal. Strong jaws break its bones. The wolves share the prey. The leads eat first.

Wolf Talk

Wolves make many sounds.

A growl says to stay away.

Wolves howl to find others.

When a pup is hungry,

it whimpers.

Wolves can smell
another pack's scent.
The smell tells them to stay
away. It's not their territory.

A wolf holds its tail high or low. This shows its rank. The leads hold their tails high. The others in the pack hold their tails lower.

Glossary

den—a place where a wild animal may live; a den may be a hole in the ground or a trunk of a tree

howl—to make a loud, sad noise

prey—an animal hunted by another animal for food

pup—a young wolf

rank—one's place within a group

territory—the land on which an animal grazes or hunts for food and raises its young

whimper—a quiet, crying noise

Read More

Bozzo, Linda. *How Wolves Grow Up*. Animals Growing Up. New York: Enslow, 2020.

Grack, Rachel. *Wolves*. North American Animals. Mankato, MN.: Amicus, 2019.

Marquardt, Meg. *Wolves on the Hunt*. Predators. Minneapolis: Lerner, 2018.

Internet Sites

Cool Kid Facts: Wolf Facts
https://www.coolkidfacts.com/wolf-facts/

International Wolf Center: Fun Wolf Facts
https://www.wolf.org/wolf-info/wild-kids/fun-facts/

San Diego Zoo: Wolf
https://animals.sandiegozoo.org/animals/wolf

Super-cool stuff! Check out projects, games, and lots more at **www.capstonekids.com**

Critical Thinking Questions

1. What animals do wolves hunt?
2. Which wolves takes care of wolf pups?
3. Name something a wolf pack does together.

Index